To

FROM Michael
with lots of love

Happy Mothers Day,
too! ●●●
Donelle

Cheryl Lynn Woods
Jaclyn Woods
Heather
Woods

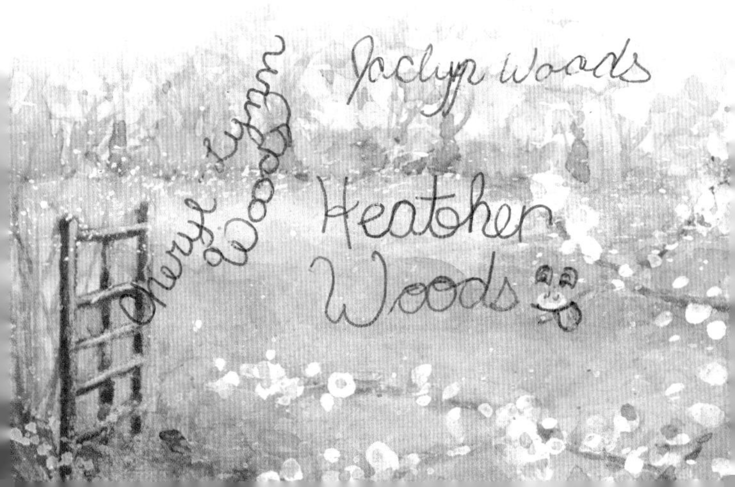

OTHER HELEN EXLEY GIFTBOOKS

For a beautiful daughter
For a super friend
For a wonderful grandchild
A Special Collection in Praise of Mothers
To a very special Mother

For my mum, who is irreplaceable.

Printed simultaneously in 2002 by Exley Publications Ltd in Great Britain
and by Exley Publications LLC in the USA.
12 11 10 9 8 7 6 5 4 3

Copyright © Helen Exley 2002
The moral right of the author has been asserted.
ISBN 1-86187-425-1

Illustrated by Juliette Clarke. Written by Siân E. Morgan.
Edited and words selected by Helen Exley. Printed in China.

Exley Publications Ltd, 16 Chalk Hill, Watford, Herts WD19 4BG, UK.
Exley Publications LLC, 185 Main Street, Spencer, MA 01562, USA.
www.helenexleygiftbooks.com

*Helen Exley Giftbooks cover the most powerful of all human
relationships: love between couples, the bonds within families and
between friends. No expense is spared in making sure that each book
is as thoughtful and meaningful a gift as it is possible to create:
good to give, good to receive. You have the result in your hands.
If you have loved it — tell others! There is no power on earth like
the word-of-mouth recommendation of friends.*

A HELEN EXLEY GIFTBOOK

For a lovely mother

Written by Siân E. Morgan
Illustrated by Juliette Clarke

▤ EXLEY

Smiles and laughter

A mother's smile alone can do so many things... the smile that tells you she's pleased to see you, the smile that says she's proud, the smile that says, "It doesn't really matter that you're untidy." And the smile that says, "It will be all right." That sympathetic, "What have you done?" smile as you limp in with a wounded knee and that soft smile as she looks at you with tear-filled eyes.

How could anyone forget that huge grin peering from the audience of your first school play, or that muffled snort when you've said something funny and your mother tries not to laugh out loud. All that noise as you both fall about laughing. And those giggles when you're both trying very hard to behave, but aren't doing a very good job....

Whenever I see your
familiar, forgiving smile, I know
that everything will be all right.

A mother believes in you

A mother thinks her child is a genius, even if no one else does.

And even if you forget your lines in the school play, fall flat on your face in a race, don't get the job, or a relationship falls apart, you don't have to pretend to be different to your mother.

She loves you just as you are, warts and all.

A mother knows all the different yous and accepts them all.

Squints, spots and bumps don't seem to matter as much to her... somehow she sees past all those things... she sees past different fashions, crazy hair dyes and changing opinions and remembers who you are.

I love it that you thought
my finger paintings were better
than Picasso and my paper mâché
blobs were better than Rodin.

Understanding each other

When no one else could understand me, you could.
You paid attention to everything I asked, you
watched closely, you anticipated, you filled in the
gaps and translated for everybody else!

We don't always need words, you and I,
Maybe all it takes is just a look.
You have always seen right through me and any
excuses I may have!

And how did you cope with all those questions
I asked (and still do!)?
All those times I asked, "Why?".
All those times I said, "But Mum..."
All those times I made impossible demands.

And how I smile every time I catch myself saying
something that you always say... and then I realize
exactly why you say it!

I love that you have been there for all those long chats, for all those times when I need your help and advice, when I'm confused, when I don't know what to do, when all around me people seem to be pushing and pulling in different ways.

Home

You could breathe life into the oldest of rooms...
or make the coldest room glow.
You could make the harshest house seem more
welcoming or make any room more comfortable.

You add your own special touches,
ornaments, pictures, photos or old drawings,
the smell of cooking or of perfume.

You can fill a room with something special,
something that can't quite be seen,
yet can be felt.
Something particular to you... that you seem
to carry with you wherever you go.

Something familiar, something safe.

IT WOULDN'T MATTER WHERE WE LIVED,
IN A HUT, A TINY FLAT OR A HUGE MANSION,
SOMEHOW YOU WOULD TURN IT INTO A HOME.

What I love best of all

I love it that you are human, just like anyone else, but that somehow you manage to do the most extraordinary things.

...That you try to put your worries, fears and problems to one side in your quest to be my protector, best friend and confidante.

That no matter what changes happen in my life, you will forever be my anchor.

I love it that you give me what you can, whenever you can
and that you do your best with what you know and what you've got at the time.

That will always be good enough for me....

No one could ever
take your place.
No one could ever replace you.
(No one else would want
the job!)

And it doesn't matter how you
love me, just that you do.
And it doesn't matter what
sort of mother you are...
just that you are mine.

I love it that you have been
able to mend bears with chewed
off ears, toys and children with
broken limbs and hurt feelings.

Is there anything
a mother can't do!

Mothers are invincible! Who could climb up a rickety tree to rescue the cat, who could see through a closed door and know what you are up to? Who could make puppets out of old socks and tents out of old sheets! Who has eyes in the back of her head!

Somehow, a mother can make a dinner stretch to feed uninvited friends and disguise the vegetables that you don't like, or can stay up to watch over you all night if you've been ill. And she can still make it through the next day.

I'm sure I'll never know about all the times when I didn't even realize you'd gone without, just to make sure that I was ok. And I know that if you had to, somehow you'd find a way to conquer the impossible.

You taught me so many things

I love that you have taught me so many things, that you repeated them with patience and care until I understood... that you hung in there long after anyone else would have given up.

You are the reason why I know my alphabet, how to tie my shoe-laces, how to be polite, that vegetables are good for me and that I should consider other people's feelings.

I love all those opportunities you gave me to learn... and made it fun. How could I forget standing on a chair watching you cook trying to be just like you... even if it drove you crazy!

And you never stop teaching me... you forever give me clues on what to do. You teach me what to say, how to cope, how to behave. You pass on to me all that life has given you.

You help me see beauty where I would not have done before... maybe just sitting and talking about nothing in particular or grabbing every moment... every drop of sun, every blustery day, every gorgeous sunset, every bit of laughter....

Somehow you manage
to find the best
in everything
and then show me.

Just being there for me

I love it every time you show that you're on my side. All those times when things don't go to plan, when you stick up for me when no one else does.

When other people thought I was too shy, too loud, too short, too fat... and you told them otherwise!

And even when I may have doubts about other people's support... I know that yours is guaranteed. That there is someone who will be thinking of me, who doesn't have any other agenda other than what they think is best for me.

And even if you were on your best adventure, or about to achieve your greatest ambition, I know you would drop everything to come to my rescue.

Just knowing that you are on the end
of the phone and willing to listen...
I love it that someone, somewhere,
has my best interests at heart.

You have always given me a second chance...

*I love it that you don't stay mad at me forever...
whether it was leaving paint splatters everywhere,
being sick on the new settee, drawing on the walls
or making a pie with all your special lipstick and
creams.*

*Or we have had arguments over anything from
clothes to borrowing the car, coming in late, not
calling, jammy fingers all over your best dress,
breaking your special vase, getting into trouble at
school, to running up a huge phone bill....*

*Or there have been disappointments about what
you wanted me to do or be. I understand that it's
usually because you want me to be safe and happy.*

We can row like crazy, slam doors, say hurtful things, wind each other up, not see eye-to-eye, go our different ways... but somehow we find a way to get back on course again.

BIG AND SMALL DISASTERS
SEEM TO FADE WITH TIME...
I LOVE IT
WHEN WE LOOK BACK ON THEM
AND LAUGH.

Knowing me, knowing you

I love it that you know exactly what makes me different to everyone else and that you love me no matter what those differences are. And how do you manage to know what I'm thinking or what I'm going to do, even before I do!

And I love that I know the real you too, not that sensible lady people see at work or in town... but the one who sat on the floor singing nursery rhymes with glitter in her hair... who tried to play football in the back yard and got covered in mud... who trampolined on the bed when she thought no one else was looking... who gets hurt by things which other people say, who worries just like everybody else, but often puts other people's concerns first. And especially mine.

All that fun...
all those adventures

I love that we have spent so much time together you and I! There have been so many happy days

...like dressing up warm on a windy, wet day and jumping in puddles, curling up on the settee with a film or a book, or racing round the play park until we made ourselves dizzy on swings and roundabouts... the sort of days when we'd chase each other round until we were both out of breath... or we put on old clothes and dug side by side in the garden.

And I'll never forget all those tickle and pillow fights when our sides hurt with laughter, silly songs in the car, that funny dance you do to make me laugh. Those are the kind of days to remember!

*I'll always remember our special
days out... when we both get excited.
And now?... I don't think
I'll ever stop looking forward
to us being together.*

All our memories

I love it that you carry memories of me around with you, that you keep all those photos and my old toys and books in the loft. I love it that you remember all the little things about me that I forget.

I love it that we have memories of us chasing around the living room pretending to be cops and robbers, sitting on the steps pretending to drive a bus... turning the kitchen table into a cave....

Whenever I feel down, I know I can think of those memories. Wherever I go, I can take those memories and will carry them with me always so that I don't feel sad or alone.

A mother's bond

I love the bond between us.
Possibly the strongest bond on earth.

...A bond that can weaken, yet be strengthened.
Which can break and yet be mended.
Which stretches to extraordinary lengths.
...A bond that allows you to be yourself and yet feel
connected. That allows you to go your own separate
way, and yet somehow never quite feel totally alone.

This is a bond that can be felt so strongly, but isn't
always visible, that can grow, even through the
worst of times, that can exist without even being
mentioned. This is a bond so powerful, that
without it, you never quite feel whole.

I love that you are as much a part of me,
as I am of you.